The Autumn Years

Insights and Reflections

The Autumn Years

Insights and Reflections

FLORENCE M. TAYLOR

The Seabury Press, New York

ACKNOWLEDGMENTS

Grateful acknowledgment is made to the following publishers and authors for permission to use copyrighted material from the titles listed:

George Allen & Unwin, Ltd., London—J. S. Hoyland, *The Light of Christ,* copyright held by Friends Home Service Committee.

Association Press, New York—Harry Emerson Fosdick, "Life's Candle Does Not Go Out," and J. G. Gilkey, "Old Age and Immortality," both in *Treasury of the Christian Faith,* ed. by Stanley I. Stuber and Thomas C. Clark.

Doubleday & Company, New York—Harold G. Henderson (ed.), *An Introduction to Haiku,* copyright © 1958 by the editor.

Harper & Row, New York—Thornton Wilder, "The Matchmaker," in *Three Plays by Thornton Wilder,* 1939 (under title "The Merchant of Yonkers"), copyright 1955, 1957, by Thornton Wilder, reprinted by permission of Brandt & Brandt; Elizabeth Gray Vining, *The World in Tune.*

The Macmillan Company, New York—Sara Teasdale, "The Coin" and "Night," in *Stars Tonight,* copyright 1930 by Sara Teasdale Filsinger, renewed 1958 by Guaranty Trust Company of New York; J. B. Phillips (trans.), *The New Testament in Modern English,* copyright © 1958, 1959, 1960, by J. B. Phillips.

The Reader's Digest Association, Pleasantville, N.J.—Mrs. Daniel W. Boyer, "Life in These United States," *The Reader's Digest,* March, 1967, copyright 1967 by the Reader's Digest Assn., Inc.

Fleming H. Revell Company, Westwood, N.J.—Hannah Whitall Smith, *The Christian's Secret of a Happy Life.*

Envied by us all,
  turning to such loveliness—
red leaves that fall.

Shiko (1664-1731), from
An Introduction to Haiku

To the Reader

✳⊹❀⊹✳⊹❀⊹✳⊹❀⊹✳⊹❀⊹✳⊹❀⊹✳⊹❀⊹✳⊹❀⊹✳⊹❀⊹✳

THIS book is being written from the vantage
point of an approaching birthday—my seventy-
fifth: seventy-five years of life, that strange, difficult, fascinating, discouraging, challenging,
baffling mystery. Life has presented generous opportunities for growth "in wisdom, and in stat-
ure, and in favor with God and men." Unrealized
opportunities they were for the most part, or why
should it still be almost impossible to apply the
results of experience to present-day situations?
This is an attempt to remind myself of some of
the things I have learned in the course of the
years, things that are peculiarly relevant to this
final stage of my life's journey.

7

"Life is short, art is long." And so hard to learn! Perhaps if life were less changeable, if the lessons learned at each stage were more easily applicable to the next development, it might prove easier. But each age, right up to the last, presents its own problems, its own difficulties, its unique lessons to be learned; and surely none are more difficult than those we find ourselves faced with in the last years of our lives. To live joyously and triumphantly at this closing stage of life is a challenge to tax spiritual strength to the utmost.

Here are no final answers, no easy solutions to the difficulties; here are only slight indications of directions in which to seek help.

If these reminders to myself may perhaps be instrumental in increasing strength and courage in others faced with similar challenges, in developing the faith that there are answers, and in encouraging others to search for their own, I shall feel well repaid for the labor of the writing.

F. M. T.

Columbus, Ohio

Contents

"We're the Old
People Now!"

WHEN I was a little girl, I overheard my mother say to her sister soon after the death of the last of my grandparents, "Liz, doesn't it seem strange—*we're* the old people now!"

I was reminded of this recently when my four-year-old grandson pointed a stubby finger at his not yet forty-year-old mother and announced positively, "Soon *she'll* be a grandmother," and added as an afterthought, "when I grow up."

Always, it seems, the recognition of each new condition, each new responsibility, comes as something of a shock. I can still remember one such moment. I was a bride of only a few weeks, adjusting to the new situation and the new responsibilities in a little four-room house. Going upstairs one morning, I glanced over my shoulder into the living room. An unfolded newspaper lay on the floor; a raincoat was thrown carelessly over a chair; the scrapbasket was overflowing.

I stood stock still, startled by a sudden realization: "This is my job. If I don't straighten up the room, *no one else* will!"

Parenthood is another responsibility that sometimes finds us ill prepared. My oldest sister, struggling with the unreasonableness of a teenage daughter, once exclaimed, penitently, to our mother, "You know, I could have been a lot better daughter if I'd been a mother first!" How true—and how sad! So many of our realizations and understandings come too late.

Looking back over the years when my mother and my husband's mother were living with us, how much more tender and understanding I could have been, *if only I could have been old first!* No amount of loving imagination can quite give the depth of understanding of a first-hand experience.

Even these late understandings need not be

totally wasted—perhaps they may make us more forgiving when younger people, who have never been old, seem to be needlessly inconsiderate or unkind. Thus we can vicariously throw back into the family life some of the tenderness and forbearance we failed to give to those long gone.

Old age, it seems to me, always comes as a complete surprise. In spite of all one's years of living, in spite of one's recognition of the passing of the years, old age itself is always a shock. One accepts the fact theoretically as the birthdays pile up, but emotionally it has no meaning. Then one day, perhaps in a department store, one sees in a mirror the image of an old, gray-haired woman passing between the counters, and with a sudden icy shock of realization, exclaims unbelievingly and ungrammatically, "Why, that's me!"

My husband describes with grim amusement one such moment of revelation. He was a sturdy, vigorous seventy at the time, and because of a heart condition had given up driving on his doctor's recommendation. He was far from immobilized, however, and thought nothing of hiking several miles. Most of the time our three-year-old grandson accompanied him, often riding in his gocart. One day they went to the hardware store on an errand, and my husband inadvertently left a small package on the counter. He went back for it later. The package was still on the counter, with a note on it: "This belongs to *the old man* with the baby carriage."

I myself tell with amusement, albeit also with a degree of tender appreciation, a similar incident that happened at a stimulating summer conference. I was over seventy and was enjoying myself tremendously. A young seminary student, not long out of his teens, showed a preference for my company that was, to say the least, flattering. He would join a group and deliberately choose to sit near me, and we had a number of brief but interesting conversations.

One day toward the end of the conference, I was sitting alone under a tree, reading, when he came over and sat beside me. For a while he did not say anything, and we sat in a companionable silence. Then he broke out impulsively, "You know, it's been wonderful, hasn't it? I mean— I guess you're the oldest person here, aren't you? And I'm the youngest. And—well—what I mean is, it's been nice knowing you!"

"Thank you," I said gently, humbly realizing that I had been given a rare gift of friendship across age barriers which often prove insurmountable.

Probably no one accepts the fact of his own old age until he sees some recognition of it reflected from those around him, but sooner or later the truth cannot be evaded or denied.

We may comfort ourselves a bit with the assurance that, as a committee member once exclaimed, "What do you mean—'the aging'? *Everybody's* aging, even a newborn baby!" But, undeniably, some of us are considerably farther along in the aging process than others.

To all of us at some time—and always, I'm sure, with a sense of shock—comes the realization: "Why! We're the old people now!"

Saturday Afternoon

❋⥵◈⥴❋⥵◈⥴❋⥵◈⥴❋⥵◈⥴❋⥵◈⥴❋⥵◈⥴❋⥵◈⥴❋⥵◈⥴❋⥵◈⥴❋⥵◈

SOME time ago there appeared in the *Reader's Digest* the following account of a true incident:

A neighbor in my Indiana home town has grown old more sweetly than anyone I've ever known. Wishing to know the secret of her poise and contentment, I said to her, "I've wondered how it feels to be 85 years old."

Her face lighted up as she replied, "Oh, it's just like Saturday afternoon on the farm, when the work is all done and you're ready for Sunday." *

What contentment and acceptance and deep,

* "Life in These United States," *Reader's Digest* (March, 1967), p. 77.

sustaining faith are reflected in those words! How one might envy that blessed octogenarian the faith that was so obviously a source of sustenance and spiritual strength in the declining years of life!

Nor is that woman a lone example. Serenely contented elderly people are to be met often— every Christian church has its shining examples of these gentle saints who have obviously accepted old age and all its discomforts and liabilities with a triumphant and gracious serenity that witnesses to the rich sufficiency of their faith.

What a pity that so many of us fight the idea of old age, resist it in spite of its inevitability, and poison the last years of living with vain regrets and bitter resentment! Why do we not instead make our own those tremendous affirmations of the Christian faith which have proved their value through generation after generation of tumultuous, tempest-torn living—those truths by which countless thousands of ordinary persons have lived triumphantly through all the vicissitudes of life and have faced the mystery of death and the hereafter serene and confident?

No two people would choose exactly the same affirmations or would express them in the same way. Each will have his unique creed, the result of his individual experience. Some of the affirmations, however, in some form, would surely appear in any Christian statement of belief. For what they may be worth, here are a few of the particular affirmations upon which my faith rests:

Thou art God!

Lord, thou hast been our dwelling place in all generations.

Before the mountains were brought forth, or ever thou hadst formed the earth and the world, even from everlasting to everlasting, thou art God.

Psalms 90:1–2 KJV

Hast thou not known? hast thou not heard, that the everlasting God, the Lord, the Creator of the ends of the earth, fainteth not, neither is weary? . . .

They that wait upon the Lord shall renew their strength; they shall mount up with wings as eagles.

Isaiah 40:28, 31 KJV

Thou art God! This is the one basic affirmation upon which rests the whole structure of our faith. We could almost stop there. So many of the other affirmations are correlative to this one. Thou art God! We can rest secure.

Thou art the Christ.

Other faiths have believed in God, but only the Christian faith defines that belief in terms of Christ. The God who is, the God who is the foundation of our faith, is identified as ". . . the Father of our Lord Jesus Christ, the Father of mercies, and the God of all comfort" (2 Cor. 1:3 KJV).

He is God as interpreted to us by the life and teaching of Jesus. He is the forgiving Father of the parable of the prodigal son (Luke 15:11–32). He is the shepherd seeking the lost and wandering sheep (Luke 15:4–7). He is the constant companion: "Lo, I am with you always" (Matt. 28:20). He is the one who claims our complete loyalty and dedication. "Thou shalt love the Lord thy God with all thy heart, and with all thy soul, and with all thy mind" (Matt. 22:37 KJV).

I am my brother's keeper.

Christianity gives no uncertain answer to the

age-old question "Am I my brother's keeper?"
(Gen. 4:9). Cain asked it, apparently fully con-
vinced that the answer would be "No, of course
not!" It is a long way from that point of view to
the declaration of the righteous Judge in Jesus'
parable of the Last Judgment:

For I was an hungered, and ye gave me no meat: I
was thirsty, and ye gave me no drink:

I was a stranger, and ye took me not in: naked, and
ye clothed me not: sick, and in prison, and ye visited
me not. . . .

Verily I say unto you, Inasmuch as ye did it not to
one of the least of these, ye did it not to me.

Matthew 25:42–43, 45 KJV

Admittedly, opportunities for service decrease
in advancing years, but they never completely
disappear.

The earth is the Lord's!

The earth is the Lord's, and the fulness thereof; the
world, and they that dwell therein. For he hath
founded it upon the seas, and established it upon the
floods.

Psalms 24:1–2 KJV

How we need to hold fast to that affirmation
today! The Christian faith approaches life with

a brave recognition of evil, but never, perhaps, has it taken more courage than it does today to affirm unconditionally: "The earth is the Lord's."

What about the incredible instruments for destruction in the hands of sometimes irresponsible governments? What about whole populations starving in a world of potential plenty? What about disease-ravaged communities where men, women, and little children are suffering and dying needlessly of diseases which present scientific knowledge could eliminate? What about a generation of young people cut adrift from age-old mores and taboos, desperately searching for new values, new anchorages? What about the thousands of Negroes in our own and other countries caught in a desperate struggle for a life of dignity and self-respect?

We look in vain for any clear answers to these and similar questions. But faith still declares, "There *is* an answer! The earth is the Lord's."

We may achieve some glimmerings of insight when we sense, however dimly, that a world without evil would also be a world totally lacking in spiritual values. Without contact with suffering, there could be no compassion; without

struggle, no triumph; without need, no response
in sacrificial service; without treachery and deceit
and hatred, no loyalty and trustworthiness and
love.

This much we may partly understand, recognizing that our knowledge and comprehension
are still microscopic compared with the vastness
of God's wisdom and the hidden scope of his
eternal purposes. Beyond this, we simply affirm:
"The earth is the Lord's . . . and they that dwell
therein."

I have sinned.

Few people live to enter the last quarter-cen-
tury of life without having a keen awareness of
sin. How seldom we hear the word nowadays,
and how we resist it when we do! But one of the
bitternesses of old age is the sudden realization
that life, with its many rich opportunities for
significant living, has narrowed down to a mere
handful of swiftly passing years. Along with
wasted opportunities, many persons look back
with bitter regret at specific acts of deliberate
or unintentional unkindness.

Trying to push these memories out of the consciousness seldom works. It is better, perhaps, to face them, to look at them in all their ugliness, and to confess, with the prodigal son: "Father, I have sinned against heaven, and in thy sight, and am no more worthy to be called thy son" (Luke 15:21 KJV).

Having made such a confession, the healthy attitude is to face forward with renewed determination to do better.

It is helpful at this point to remember Peter and Judas. Both sinned shamefully against their beloved master. Judas never grasped the comfort of confession and forgiveness—he killed himself. Peter, however, "wept bitterly"—then took up his life with renewed determination and lived it to a triumphant conclusion.

I will fear no evil.

I will *fear* no evil—not old age, not suffering, not illness, not loneliness, not bereavement, not death! I will *fear* no evil. Why? *Not* because God's goodness and protective care will prevent evil from happening to me. Evil happens to everyone; it is an inescapable part of life. I will fear no evil *because* "Thou art with me." God's continuing presence and companionship make it possible to meet the worst that life can bring with acceptance and triumphant courage.

I will rejoice.

Lack of fear is good; rejoicing is better. Happiness is not an accidental occurrence due to outward circumstances; it is an inner achievement, the inevitable result of a right relationship to God and to his people.

This is the day which the Lord hath made; we will rejoice and be glad in it.

Psalm 118:24 KJV

I am come that they might have life, and that they might have it more abundantly.

John 10:10 KJV

How does it feel to be old? "Like Saturday afternoon on the farm, when the work is all done and you're ready for Sunday"? Yes—if you have made the tremendous affirmations of the Christian faith your own. "Be happy in your faith at all times." *

* I Thessalonians 5:16a, from J. B. Phillips, trans., *The New Testament in Modern English* (New York: Macmillan, 1958).

Preparation for Retirement

I SHALL always be grateful to my doctor for some advice he gave me one day, quite casually and incidentally.

It was several years before I would be faced with compulsory retirement from a job in which I was thoroughly engrossed. It was a demanding job and a challenging one, and I loved every minute of it.

I was in the doctor's office for a routine checkup when he asked casually, apropos of nothing that had gone before, "What are you going to do when you retire?"

I looked at him in surprise. "Why, I don't

know," I answered. "I haven't thought much about it." (Who ever does?) After a moment, I went on thoughtfully, "I'll probably continue to do some writing, and sometimes I have a feeling I'd like to pick up my piano playing again."

"Good," he said, and then added positively (he was a *very* positive person!), "The time to get ready to retire is *now*, before it happens. You sign up right away for some piano lessons and get started."

"But I haven't time," I protested. "You know I'm working every day and several nights a week. I haven't time now to practice. Later on, perhaps."

"Nonsense!" he exclaimed. "You'll find the time for anything you're interested in. You begin to pick up your music right now."

It was an order! Moreover, the more I thought about it, the better sense it made. I was not then, nor am I now, an accomplished pianist. I had very little instruction, but the few hours I had spent at the piano from time to time had been enjoyable and I had found real pleasure in playing duets with my talented daughter—I doing

the easy bass chords and she providing the spectacular treble.

On an impulse, that same evening I called up
my daughter's former teacher, then retired, and
received an enthusiastic response to my somewhat
hesitant proposal for some lessons. And so for
several years, somewhat irregularly but on the
whole fairly steadily, I spent many spare minutes
at the piano.

And how it has paid off! I live now in the
midst of a musical family. My modest musical
training is providing an interest that ties me in
with the family life. Sometimes it is my fifteen-
year-old grandson, a budding violinist, who calls,
"Gay-Gay, how about practicing with me?"
Sometimes it is one of the girls (or more rarely
their mother) who suggests, "Let's play some
duets." Often it is the five-year-old grandson:
"Listen to me play 'Chopsticks'!" And once in
a while, when we have a rare evening alone, my
husband will say, "How about some music just
for me?"

Even now it is a rare day that goes by without
my spending some time at the piano. Arthritic

hands interfere with difficult technique, but much simple and satisfying music is still within the range of my ability.

How often I have remembered and been grateful for my doctor's advice: "The time to get ready for retirement is before it happens." Of course, it is not impossible to pick up on hobbies and interests after retirement, but having some already started acts as a bridge and provides an immediate occupation to give meaning to the changed days.

For some people, instrumental music of some kind may prove "just what the doctor ordered." For others, an accumulated shelf of books is an excellent device. Here you may store away, right at your elbow, the particular books you have wanted to read but did not, for lack of time.

For still others, some ambitious handwork project may serve the purpose—a knitted or crocheted afghan, perhaps, lovely enough to be a family heirloom, or an old-fashioned crocheted bedspread, or a set of crewel-embroidered chair seats. One man started a spectacular dolls' house, with separate switches to light individual rooms, for his granddaughters.

The idea is to cultivate at least one hobby outside the area of your regular occupation, long before you face the sudden idleness of retirement that frequently breeds discontent. The busy older person usually finds contentment.

Accepting Old Age

DO all old people, I wonder, react, as I do, with considerable irritation to the sentimental approach to old age? This is no time, it seems to me, for sentimentality, for closing the eyes to facts, for soft-pedaling the realities of existence. On the contrary, it is a time when what is most needed is courage enough to look the facts in the face. Old age means loss of economic status, decreasing physical strength, waning energy, contracting circles of activity, gradual loss of power and influence, increasing ill health, pain, suffering, loneliness, bereavement, and the imminence of death. Quite a list of grim realities to face up to!

All three dimensions of life—past, present and future—sometimes seem shrouded in a mist of gloom.

No matter how happy the past may have been, dwelling on its memories now may produce a deep discontent with the contrasting present. Some of us, moreover, carry a burden of regret for wasted opportunities, for unfulfilled dreams and resolves, for neglected kindnesses and a few deliberate unkindnesses, for unforgivable indifference to the sufferings of others, for failure to respond to the human need constantly revealed to us on every side.

As for the present, most of us find ourselves in a peripheral position. Loss of power and responsibility is hard to take. People who in their active years were involved in important tasks, feeling the challenge of great opportunities, using their fine creative abilities to solve difficulties and project new undertakings, often find themselves in old (and not so old) age suddenly in the position of observers, looking on from the sidelines, no longer sharing in the power and responsibility of important affairs, their opinions no longer sought, their suggestions brushed aside as unimportant and irrelevant.

No one can deny that this is hard to accept. Not to be needed is very often fatal to a person's self-esteem. But just as the mother must learn to see her finest achievement as the independence of her child, his maturity proved by his ability to do without her, so as old age comes on, genuine acceptance of a peripheral position in life is one of the necessities of a wholesome adjustment.

So much for the past and the present. What about the future? Suddenly the future has almost ceased to exist. No longer does it stretch endlessly ahead, full of all kinds of challenging opportunities and delightful possibilities. Suddenly, it just isn't there—or at least it is so uncertain that the only real certainty is its not-too-distant termination.

These are the facts—hard, unpleasant, unavoidable—that must be faced if we are to live victoriously and triumphantly through these final months and years of life.

It may be helpful to recall that every stage of life, when we were in the midst of it, presented a similar catalogue of gloom. It is only in retrospect that childhood, and perhaps adolescence, seem carefree and happy. And surely a moment's honest reflection will lead us to admit that in our busiest, mature years there were times when we would gladly have shed some of our responsibilities for some much-longed-for leisure.

It seems that each stage of life has its inevitable difficulties and, as surely, its compensations. The protected baby, as safe as human love can make him, still needs to protest and struggle to find himself. The adolescent, surrounded by a supportive family, has to break loose from what seems like unbearable restraint in order to realize his own capabilities. And the mature man or woman, overburdened by responsibilities apparently beyond his strength, perhaps needs that very overload in order, through the struggle, to realize his own potential.

And what about us now—those of us who have developed through all these stages with varying degrees of success? At every preceding stage, struggle has been an integral part of the pattern of life, bringing with it greater abilities, new strengths, new understandings. But now there is

a difference. Struggle against the particular difficulties of old age will get us nowhere. No amount
of struggling against physical weakness and lack
of energy will make us one whit stronger or more
energetic. It will only spill gloom to darken the
present.

Nor will any struggle against the future change
it. No resisting the imminence of death is going
to postpone it by one second.

In this final stage of our lives, *struggle gets us
nowhere*. We have to find a new technique for
overcoming our difficulties, a whole new pattern
for our lives. I have always loved the comment of
Carlyle about the woman who declared, "I accept
the universe!" His terse reply was "Gad! She'd
better!"

There is a parallel here for us. Just as struggle
was the key word in our earlier stages of life, just
as it was necessary for our survival and matura-
tion, so there is a key word for our old age: *acceptance*.

Positive acceptance of old age as it is, with no
denying of its difficulties, with no shutting our
eyes to any of its undesirable aspects—this is the
new technique for us to learn.

"We accept old age!" "Gad! We'd better!" We have no other real choice. Only after acceptance can we go on to discover that in this age, as in all the others, surprising compensations come. Only then can we begin to cultivate those gracious skills of living that are peculiarly fitting for old age.

Expanding Circles— and Contracting

EACH of us inevitably seems to himself, much of the time, to be the center of the universe. From the moment when our awakening consciousness becomes aware of our surroundings, our life develops in widening circles—from the close confinement of the mother's womb to the only slightly less protective encirclement of her arms, on out into the home surroundings, and then in widening circles of consciousness into the community, the country, the world, and finally into awareness of the illimitable universe of which we are a part.

Developing human beings respond in various ways to these new areas of experience and activity.

Some meet them with a feeling of uneasiness and discomfort; each expanding area presents a threat, each new experience becomes something to dread. Others are able to welcome the new and the strange with a sense of anticipation and delight in adventure.

The attitude of joyous expectancy has a great deal to do with successful adjustment to new situations, new responsibilities. The child going to school, the young person going away to college, the man or woman entering the world of business or profession, the bride and groom starting their life together—all these are helped by an attitude of confidence and joy.

Surely this is also true of all of us as we approach the closing years of our lives. It is easy, but profoundly unwise, to accept our modern society's valuation of old age as a time of idleness and senility, as years of inactivity and boredom.

True it is that at some point in our development there comes the realization that the expanding circles of our physical existence have reversed their direction, have begun to contract again, closer and closer, until for many of us at last they have narrowed to the dimensions of a single

room. This much we must accept. But it is also
true that some rare souls seem able to cope with
the reality of the contracting physical circles
without suffering a diminution of their spiritual
interests and concerns. They are the dauntless
ones who witness to the truth that "Stone walls
do not a prison make,/Nor iron bars a cage"
(Richard Lovelace [1618–58]).

Theoretically, at least, the widening spiritual
circles continue indefinitely. How beautifully
Oliver Wendell Holmes has expressed this idea
in his "The Chambered Nautilus":

Year after year beheld the silent toil
  That spread his lustrous coil;
  Still, as the spiral grew,
He left the past year's dwelling for the new,
Stole with soft step its shining archway through,
  Built up its idle door,
Stretched in his last-found home, and knew the old
          no more.

Build thee more stately mansions, O my soul,
  As the swift seasons roll!
  Leave thy low-vaulted past.
Let each new temple, nobler than the last,
Shut thee from heaven with a dome more vast,

Till thou at length art free,
Leaving thine outgrown shell by life's unresting
sea.

Surely the building of "more stately mansions"
must not cease with the years of lessened physical
activity. What finer concern could engage our
hearts and minds during these years than the
gradual escape from our "low-vaulted past" into
that greater freedom which sees even death itself
as a joyous adventure of faith?

The rightness and wholesomeness of this attitude seems obvious. Our hearts and minds expand
to greater awareness, greater depths of understanding, greater and more spiritual insights,
until, perhaps (who knows?), we emerge from
this physical existence into some unguessed realization of freedom and truth and eternal joyous
activity in dimensions far exceeding our finite
human understandings.

The "Poor Me's"

I HAD an old auntie who used to shake her head sadly over my querulous complaints and murmur, "My, oh my! You surely do have a bad case of the 'poor me's.'"

"Poor me! I haven't anything to do!" "Poor me! Nobody likes me." "Poor me! Why do I have to go to bed *now?*" "Poor me! Do I *have* to dry the dishes?"

Children are not the only ones who develop bad cases of the "poor me's." It is a disease especially liable to attack old people.

"Poor me! I never slept a wink all night!" "Poor me! Everybody mumbles nowadays." "Poor me! Nobody wants me around." "Poor me! My arthritis is almost unbearable." And so on and on and on.

"Good morning, Grandma. How are you to-day?" is *not* an invitation to a long description of aches and pains. What is indicated is a cheerful "Fine, thanks." Or if you have a sensitive conscience that objects to this as an untruth, perhaps you can recognize that this is a rhetorical question that needs no direct answer, and contrive a truthful response that changes the subject. "Good morning! What a lovely day!" or "Good morning! That was quite a storm last night."

All of which in no sense denies the justification for the "poor me's." It *is* miserable to toss and turn, sleepless, hour after hour. It *is* hard to stand the constant gnawing minor (or major) pains of arthritis. To be in the midst of a group and unable to hear what people say, or to half-hear and miss the punch line of the joke or the crux of the conversation, is an exasperating experience. I do not know a single old person who could not describe a list of complaints that would be reason enough to make a saint gloomy.

Only the saints never are gloomy. They are the rare souls who live joyously and triumphantly in the midst of all their sufferings. They are the blessed ones who spread the contagion of mental health and happiness. Theirs is a skill of living well worth acquiring at any age, especially in old age—the ability to master and control our gloomy emotions.

Psychologists tell us that emotion produces action, but also that action produces emotion. We are afraid, and so we run away. But equally true is the fact that we are afraid *because* we run away.

Act as though you are happy—and you'll *be* happy. Smile—and some of the gloom will be dissipated. Count your blessings—and suddenly you will find true gratitude welling up in your heart. Act as though you are unafraid—and genuine courage will take you by surprise.

This mastery of our coward moods would be far less important if it were a matter which concerned only our own happiness or unhappiness. But this is never true. Mood contagion is a tremendously powerful force.

A tired, discouraged mother creates in her children the very tensions and irritabilities which cause her tiredness. A gloomy grandparent, grumping and complaining, can spread the contagion of ill humor through the whole family and completely dissipate the normal, happy atmosphere of the family life.

"But I can't *always* be happy!" No, of course not. Who does not sometimes need the release from tension that "a good cry" brings? But at least when those times come, we can cry by ourselves, in secret. We would never deliberately expose our family or those around us to the infection of a contagious disease; but the contagion of unhappiness, of ill humor, of gloominess and bitterness is well-nigh irresistible.

Share your joy, but hide your sorrow. Share your faith, but hide your doubt. Share your love, pour it out liberally through every personal contact—freely, ungrudgingly, asking nothing in return. And rejoice that love, too, is irresistibly contagious. One truly loving person can sweeten and restore innumerable broken relationships.

Love is patient and kind . . .
Love does not insist on its own way; it is not irritable **or** resentful . . .
Love bears all things . . .
Make love your aim.

A Dried Oak Leaf

❋↝۞↗❋↝۞↗❋↝۞↗❋↝۞↗❋↝۞↗❋↝۞↗❋↝۞↗❋↝۞↗❋↝۞

ONE of the causes of unhappiness in the latter years of life is that of bereavement. Whether it is the death of a mate, of a member of the family, or of a dearly loved friend, the feeling of emptiness created by the passing of a loved one is surely one of life's most difficult experiences.

It is easy to meet this trial by a withdrawal, by a turning away from other, perhaps less dear relationships, by a mood of bitter self-pity.

In Thornton Wilder's *The Matchmaker,* a woman who has lost her husband recounts her reaction:

Yes, in the evenings, I'd put out the cat, and I'd lock the door, and I'd make myself a little rum toddy;

and before I went to bed I'd say a little prayer, thanking God that I was independent—that no one else's life was mixed up with mine.

So far, this is a fairly typical reaction—of withdrawal, of turning inward in response to the hurt. But listen to the rest of her comment:·

And one night after two years an oak leaf fell out of my Bible—a perfectly good oak leaf—but without color and without life. Suddenly I realized that for a long time I had not shed one tear; nor had I been filled with the wonderful hope that something or other would turn out well. I saw that I was like that oak leaf, and on that night I decided to rejoin the human race.

No, retreating from life has no healing in it; rather, what is needed is a deep thanksgiving for the companionship which has so richly blessed our lives, a renewed appreciation of remaining human ties of affection, a reaching out for new warm relationships, a genuine involvement in the lives of those about us.

"It's Their Turn Now!"

※⤳✦⤳✦⤳✦⤳✦⤳✦⤳✦⤳✦⤳✦⤳✦⤳✦⤳✦⤳✦⤳✦

SOME of my pleasantest memories are con-
nected with Grandma Taylor's cottage at the
seashore. By the side of the house, a fine, long
swing hung between two huge upended logs.

All the children and young people of the community used the swing as if it were their own
with almost complete freedom. Grandma was
never far away; and whenever a dispute arose as
to whose turn it was, suddenly she would appear,
usually to chase away the older ones so that the
smaller ones might have their turn.

Three-year-old Ruthie, who lived a few houses
away, soon learned who her champion was.
Whenever she arrived at the swing, no matter

how many children were there ahead of her, she would take one look, toddle over to the cottage door, pound with her chubby fist, and sing-song over and over until Grandma appeared: " 'Tayl', my tu'n! 'Tayl', my tu'n!"

"It's my turn now!" How old was I, I wonder, when I first heard or used that imperious demand? What a long and difficult task it is to learn the fairness and necessity of taking turns! Do we ever really learn it? Isn't it true that at the end of three-quarters of a century we are still resisting its inevitable imperative?

For years it was our turn to hold positions of leadership and influence and authority. But now it is the turn of others.

Why does the important executive resent the younger assistant with new and different ideas?

That committee of the church or club that we organized and led for several years, that took so much of our time and energy—why is it so terribly hard to let go of the responsibility, to stand aside with warm encouragement and *no interference* while others try out their ideas?

And these children of ours, long since grown up—once they were completely subject to our control, even on such details as to what they wore and ate, and what time they went to bed. Now these children are mature individuals with children of their own. *It's their turn now* to decide what their children do. Why should we be so outraged if they decide that their children may be permitted or denied privileges that are different from those we used? *It's their turn now.*

Perhaps one of the skills we most need to acquire in old age is the ability to recognize that *we've had our turn.*

"Look for a Lovely Thing"

TO my father I owe an awareness of beauty that is one of the indestructible pleasures of living. Old age is powerless to eradicate it. Even fading eyesight cannot totally deprive me—there is always memory.

Sara Teasdale has given inspired expression to the value of remembered beauty:

> Oh, better than the minting
> Of a gold-crowned king
> Is the safe-kept memory
> Of a lovely thing.*

* "The Coin," in *Stars Tonight* (New York: Macmillan, 1930).

Three memories of lovely things stand out from the early days of childhood, all three associated with my father.

The earliest one dates from the time when I was perhaps four years old. I was lying half awake one morning in early spring. Suddenly my father was bending over me.

"I want to show you something," he said, and lifting me in his strong arms, he carried me to a window in another room. "Look!" he said. "Look at the pear tree!"

In wonder I gazed at the tree. The early rays of sunlight flashed upon living bits of color all over its branches—a whole flock of migrating warblers had paused in their long flight and had been our unsuspected overnight guests. And to the jewel-like beauty of the tiny feathered forms was added the loveliness of their morning songs of praise.

Breathless, we watched and listened, until as though at a given signal, the flock whirred aloft and winged their way onward.

The second incident also happened in the early morning. This time it was a glorious sunrise that

I was lifted from my bed to enjoy. The sky, from the eastern horizon to the zenith, was covered with fluffy, broken gray clouds—and each was edged with vivid crimson.

The third memory is of a time when my father and I were walking along the Jersey seashore. It was low tide, and the mighty ocean that had been huge, raging billows a few hours earlier was now almost as still as a lake. Small, lazy waves, scarcely more than ripples, rolled up across the sand and flowed gently back again, leaving the wet sand smooth and firm beneath our bare feet. And then, as one wave receded, the sand was suddenly alive with hundreds of little living sea creatures, each no more than half an inch long and a quarter of an inch wide, enclosed in two tiny "sunrise" shells—shells of pale pink, pale yellow, pale lavender, rayed like the radiant morning sky, each lovelier than the last—a glory of exquisite, miniature creations. What could one do but stand still and think of the wonders of God?

Sensitivity to beauty in its myriad forms is one blessing old age cannot take from us. Sara Teasdale's advice in the following brief poem is good for anyone, but is especially appropriate for us oldsters:

> Stars over snow,
>   And in the west a planet
> Swinging below a star—
>   Look for a lovely thing and you will find it,
> It is not far
>   It never will be far.*

Should we cultivate this sensitivity to beauty merely because of the aesthetic enjoyment it provides? Surely there is a deeper reason. Such moments bring us close to the mystery at the center of life.

There is an hour of the Indian night, a little before the first glimmer of dawn, when the stars are unbelievably clear and close above, shining with a radiance beyond our belief in this foggy land. The trees stand silent around one with a friendly presence. As yet there is no sound from awakening birds; but the whole world seems to be intent, alive, listening, eager. At such a moment the veil between the things that are seen and the things that are unseen becomes so thin as to interpose scarcely any barrier at all between

* "Night," *ibid*.

the eternal beauty and truth and the soul which would
comprehend them.**

** J. S. Hoyland, *The Light of Christ* (London: George
Allen & Unwin, 1928).

Fearfully and
Wonderfully Made

✻⟿❂⟿✻⟿❂⟿✻⟿❂⟿✻⟿❂⟿✻⟿❂⟿✻⟿❂⟿✻⟿❂⟿✻⟿❂

Lord, I am fearfully and wonderfully made.
Psalms 139:14 KJV

THE unknown psalmist who first caught this insight impearled it for the benefit of following generations in these words.

"Fearfully and wonderfully made," indeed! The marvel of our bodies is one most of us take thoughtlessly for granted. Few stop to wonder as the ancient psalmist did. One of the few who did, voiced his wonder in a prayer:

Is not sight a jewel? Is not hearing a treasure? Is not speech a glory? O my Lord, pardon my ingratitude, and pity my dullness who am not sensible of these gifts. The freedom of Thy bounty hath deceived me.

59

These things were too near to be considered. Thou presentedst me with Thy blessings, and I was not aware. But now I give thanks and adore and praise Thee for Thine inestimable favors.*

Thomas Traherne (?1637–1674)

Sight, hearing, and speech are only three of many marvels in these bodies which we inhabit more or less precariously for a term of years. Think of the steady pulsing of the heart year after year after year. Think of all the complicated processes that take place in the digestive system. Think of the amazing healing and recuperating powers. Usually the only time we are aware of these miracles is when we complain of their occasional malfunctioning.

My particular favorite among the body miracles is the human hand. What a peculiarly effective instrument it is for carrying out our purposes! How constantly our hands are busy ministering to our own and others' needs, improving our environment, bringing gardens to lovely flowering, giving voices to musical instruments.

* In Barbara Greene and Victor Gollancz, *God of a Hundred Names* (Garden City, N.Y.: Doubleday, 1963).

And all these things are accomplished with almost complete unawareness on our part—until we cut a finger, or until the crippling of arthritis suddenly makes us conscious of our loss of dexterity.

Were we creatures without hands, suddenly endowed with them, how we should marvel at their usefulness! Surely such amazing tools should be used sacramentally.

Even arthritic hands need not be despised— they are still capable of sacramental use. I had a dear aunt who, for years before her death, was constantly knitting for the Red Cross. Literally dozens of sweaters were made by her aged, twisted fingers, and dozens of disaster victims were grateful for her anonymous ministry. And in countless three-generation homes, as in previous centuries, the misshapen hands of the aged still perform almost continuous loving acts of service—washing dishes, mending clothes, comforting the hurts of toddlers.

Nor is this ministry limited to women. Men, too, have their special abilities to contribute. How many loved toys have come from the home workshops of grandfathers! How many broken toys have been mended, how many articles of furniture reconditioned! How many small boys have exclaimed with conviction, "Gosh! Granddad can fix *anything!*"

"Christ has no hands but our hands," sang a poet in a moment of insight. We may be grateful indeed that across the world, even with its present weight of woe, hundreds and thousands of hands are dedicated to doing "his work" today.

It is still true that so long as we live and breathe, some portion of that work will remain undone, some bit of God's purpose for some of his creatures will be unfulfilled, unless we, who have passed our years of greatest usefulness, still offer him hearts sensitive to the needs of those around us, minds alert to opportunities of possible service, and hands (and tongues) dedicated to the doing of his will.

Minor Ecstasies

✳✦◉↗✳✦◉↗✳✦◉↗✳✦◉↗✳✦◉↗✳✦◉↗✳✦◉↗✳✦◉↗✳✦◉↗✳✦◉

ELIZABETH Gray Vining has described some of the deeply joyous experiences of life as "minor ecstasies." She writes:

Only a few people, and those few but infrequently, know ecstasy. It is a big word; it means a state of being outside oneself and outside time, caught up in an overwhelming emotion; it implies a high occasion and a greatness of response to it. Mystics have used the word to express the ineffable joy of union with Reality, the flight, in Plotinus' phrase, of the alone to the Alone; it applies to the selfless raptures of human love and parenthood, to what artists feel when what they create seems to be coming through them from something beyond. With such grandeurs of experience, alps towering above the plain of daily living, I am not now concerned. I am thinking of what I have learned to call minor ecstasies, bits of star dust which are for all of us, however monotonous our days and cramped our lives, however limited our opportunities.*

"Minor ecstasies" is a happy phrase. Everyone has a few memories of such moments—brief flickers of intense joy—gone almost before they are recognized, but so intense that they remain forever living memories capable of being recalled instantly, with something of the original magic still lingering.

I remember one such moment. I was struggling to regain my balance after a sudden ending to my first love affair. Love had always been a taken-for-granted experience, and it had not seemed *too* miraculous to be the object of this special kind of love; it had been quite natural and expected. But then came the unnatural and unexpected ending. Such a pitiful ending—nothing great or tragic, not the death of the loved one on a battlefield or anything at all dramatic, just the realization on his part that he did not love me

* Elizabeth Gray Vining, *The World in Tune* (New York: Harper & Row, 1954), pp. 27–28.

after all. My pride and self-esteem were shattered. My world had come tumbling down like a house of cards.

But life went on. And one night a few weeks later, I was walking alone up a country road to the school where I was a resident teacher. And as I walked, sunk deep in my misery, I suddenly lifted my head. I saw the outline of the hills against the starry sky, and into my mind flashed the words "I will lift up mine eyes unto the hills, from whence cometh my help. My help cometh from the Lord, which made heaven and earth" (Ps. 121:1,2 KJV).

I stood still in the dark road, my face lifted to the hills, and suddenly, with a swift upsurge of joy, I knew that help had come. A sense of strength and power flooded through me; and I stood transfixed, drawing deep breaths of spiritual renewal, before I finally went on up the hill.

A "minor ecstasy," a "bit of star dust," as vivid today in memory as though it had happened only yesterday, instead of fifty-five years ago—far more vivid than the memory of the need which called it forth.

Another minor ecstasy comes to mind. This

one happened only three years ago. I had been away for several weeks and had just alighted from the return plane. As I started down the long passageway from the gate, I caught sight of my family far ahead. At the same minute my three-year-old grandson saw me, broke away from his mother's hand, and came racing down the passageway, shrieking at the top of his lungs, "Gay-Gay! Gay-Gay!" Amused passengers moved aside to give him room, and several turned to see the lucky recipient of such an enthusiastic welcome. I stopped and braced myself for his onslaught, and caught him to me with a depth of joy that can truly be described as ecstatic.

Love, the greatest miracle in existence—how often we take it entirely for granted! We do well to accept it humbly, with awe and reverence, and with ecstatic response whenever we are its object.

These "minor ecstasies" from the past are memories to be frequently recalled and relived. They renew our faith in the goodness of life, strengthen our belief in the possibility of more ecstatic experiences, and increase our ability to recognize and savor them when they occur.

Misers of Time

"I CAN'T wait till next week!" "I wish my birthday would hurry up and come!" "How long *now* until Christmas?"

With such heedless prodigality does youth wish away time! Not so with us oldsters. It may be true that we are anticipating something that will happen next week, or next month, or next year. (Seldom do we dare look much beyond that.) But *in the meantime* we treasure the days with miserly thrift.

At long last we have learned fully to appreciate the Sanskrit "Salutation to the Dawn":

Look well to this day! For it is life.
The very life of life.

In its brief course lie all the verities
And realities of your existence:
  The bliss of growth,
  The glory of action,
  The splendor of beauty:
For yesterday is but a dream,
And tomorrow is only a vision,
  But today, well-lived,
Makes every yesterday a dream of happiness,
And every tomorrow a vision of hope.
  Look well, therefore, to this day.

                              Kalidasa (c. 500)

Last Christmas I opened a small package and unrolled a cloth calendar, a lovely thing of soft browns, muted reds, and gold, with a Bible verse painted on the cloth: "This is the day which the Lord hath made; we will rejoice and be glad in it" (Ps. 118:24 KJV).

"Oh," I exclaimed, "that's one of my favorite Bible verses!"

"I know," said my twelve-year-old granddaughter, nodding her head. "That's why I got it for you. I thought of you the minute I saw it."

The calendar has hung on my wall all year, a constant reminder that happiness is a spiritual

achievement, not the result of fortuitous circumstances.

What are the things that prevent us from living
today to the fullest? Sometimes, it is true, present
factors are largely responsible for our discontent
—physical discomfort, loneliness, boredom. These
need to be overcome by a special effort to change
our mood, perhaps by immersing ourselves,
through an effort of will, in some congenial activity, perhaps by a general mental houseclean-
ing that sweeps out the gloomy cobwebs of discontent and allows the cheery thoughts of God's
manifest blessings to crowd our minds.

Often, however, in addition to the day's legiti-
mate difficulties, yesterday and tomorrow cast
their ugly shadows across what could be the
bright gladness of today. Too many of us spend
our days in useless repining over happy yester-
days now gone (instead of being grateful for such
happy memories) or in dreading the future, wor-
rying about calamities that, often, never happen.

Hannah Whitall Smith tells a pertinent anec-
dote, reminding us first that there is Scriptural
authority for this emphasis on living in the pres-

ent. For we are commanded: "Take therefore no thought for the morrow: for the morrow shall take thought for the things of itself. Sufficient unto the day is the evil thereof" (Matt. 6:34 KJV).

She goes on to tell about a poor household drudge, "a woman who earned a precarious living by daily labor, but who was a joyous triumphant Christian":

"Ah, Nancy," said a gloomy Christian lady to her one day, who almost disapproved of her constant cheerfulness, and yet envied it,—"Ah, Nancy, it is all well enough to be happy now, but I should think the thoughts of your future would sober you. Only suppose, for instance, that you should have a spell of sickness, and be unable to work; or suppose your present employers should move away, and no one else should give you anything to do; or suppose—" "Stop!" cried Nancy, "I never supposes. De Lord's my Shepherd, and I knows I shall not want. And, honey," she added to her gloomy friend, "it's all dem *supposes* as is making you so mis'able. You'd better give dem all up, and just trust de Lord." *

The fewer days we have left, the more we

* Hannah W. Smith, *The Christian's Secret of a Happy Life* (Westwood, N.J.: Fleming H. Revell, 1952), pp. 149–150.

should fill them to the brim with the happiness that comes from a right relationship to God and to our neighbors, with a grateful recognition of "minor ecstasies" that have been ours in the past, with an upwelling gratitude for present blessings, and with a peaceful acceptance of whatever lies ahead.

Good Company for Myself

✻⁕❀⁕✻⁕❀⁕✻⁕❀⁕✻⁕❀⁕✻⁕❀⁕✻⁕❀⁕✻⁕❀⁕✻⁕❀⁕✻⁕❀

A FRIEND of mine in her eighties spent much of her time alone. "Lonely?" she used to reply to inquirers. "Oh, no! I'm very good company for myself." What a tremendously valuable skill of living, the ability to be good company for oneself!

Surely this ability comes, first of all, from a basically wholesome self-regard—a realization of oneself as an interesting and likable person. A person characterized by feelings of inferiority, a sense of failure, anxieties, and bitterness would find it difficult to achieve such contentment.

The contented older person has usually achieved an optimistic thought trend that finds genuine enjoyment in the uneventful passing days, consciously appreciates simple pleasures, quietly savors moments of beauty, joyously recalls "minor ecstasies," and faces the future serene and unafraid.

In addition to all this, the contented older person is almost invariably a busy person, one who has cultivated many interests and abilities, and fills his days with pleasurable activities.

For the years of lessened physical activity, countless and varied opportunities for enjoying "aloneness" are available.

READING: This stands high on my personal list of devices for overcoming loneliness. The contracting circles of physical existence are powerless to confine the mind; and one of the compensations of old age is that now we have time to read what we want to, free from the demands of reading almost exclusively in the narrow limits of occupation or profession. Now we can reach out and sample all the rich areas of literature—biography, philosophy, fiction, poetry, drama. How fortunate we are to live in a country where libraries are usually as convenient as grocery stores!

RECORDS: Closely related to books, records

provide another source of easily acquired pleasure. How about a study of Shakespeare? Readings of his plays by skillful actors are available at most record libraries. More and more records of other books are becoming available. What a boon for those whose failing eyesight makes reading difficult!

And of course the whole world of music can be brought into the narrow limits of your own room, even a sickroom. You have only to make your own selection. How about a detailed study of one favorite composer? The librarian would be glad to suggest biographical and critical commentaries to aid you.

TELEVISION: This seems less valuable to me than the items previously mentioned because it is so much less flexible and adaptable to personal interests, but as a means of escaping loneliness it has its uses. Certainly the news broadcasts make any feeling of isolation impossible, and isn't it surprising what a feeling of companionship and intimacy (even though one-sided) you develop toward your favorite broadcaster?

LETTER-WRITING: This is an excellent device for overcoming loneliness and an opportunity for us oldsters to chatter to our hearts' content. Few recipients ever complain that letters are too long!

In this mobile age, many of us find ourselves separated from friends and relatives, but distance need not destroy the ties of friendship that have endured for many years.

Most of us look forward to the influx of mail at Christmas time with genuine anticipation. The family letters and photographs, the brief scrawled messages, even the cards with just a signature, all combine to spread a network of friendly ties that gives us a warm sense of manifold relationships.

These friendly greetings, however, need not be limited to Christmas. Each one of us surely knows the joy of the letter from a dearly loved old friend that comes unexpectedly and for no apparent reason. We could provide reasons for more frequent contacts.

One device is to set aside a special time each week to be devoted to letter-writing. This is a two-edged technique for combating loneliness— the writing of the letter itself and the delight of receiving an answer.

A DIARY: Did you keep a diary when you

were an adolescent? I did, and I remember what a safety valve it was for me to be able to confide in it all my innermost wonderings and doubts and feelings, things I would not have told even my best friend. Admittedly, this has its dangers, but it is surely less dangerous than bottling up feelings that may someday explode. Explode them harmlessly in a diary, and avoid the risk of hurt feelings and strained relationships.

SOLITAIRE AND PUZZLES: "Do *you* play solitaire?" my friends sometimes ask in surprise. And I am almost hesitant to admit that I find solitaire a completely satisfactory substitute for a table of bridge. I am far less likely to be annoyed by myself than by the stupidities and irritating habits of many card players I have known! And it is easier to stop when I've had enough.

Another of my favorite relaxations is doing puzzles. I like them all—crossword, Double-Crostics, even jigsaws.

OCCUPATIONAL THERAPY: When I was growing up, no one, I think, had ever heard of "occupational therapy," but my mother knew all about the danger of Satan's finding mischief for idle hands, and so we girls acquired a number of skills for which I have been exceedingly grateful. My mother was an expert needlewoman, and we were introduced at various times to many forms of sewing—hemstitching, featherstitching, smocking, embroidery—to knitting, crocheting, beadwork, rugmaking (braided and hooked), and even to leatherwork and woodburning. So we early learned the joy of creative arts and crafts.

Nowadays the psychological value of such occupations is widely recognized, and men as well as women find enjoyment in painting, clay modeling, copper tooling, and similar pastimes.

SERVICE ACTIVITIES: Occupations that are tied in with some form of service have an additional element of enjoyment. These overcome loneliness by establishing ties (anonymous but real) to the needy ones of the world.

Do you remember how during the war groups of women found deep satisfaction and fulfillment in folding bandages and knitting for the Red Cross? Something of the same satisfaction is available even to the shut-in, who finds, perhaps in connection with her church's mission program, a project which can make good use of her time and abilities—knitting afghans or baby blankets, or making bandages for lepers, for example.

Surely, with so many opportunities for happy, worthwhile occupation, each of us should be able to find the activities which enable us to declare: "Lonely? Oh, no! I'm very good company for myself." Amen and amen.

Three-Generation Homes

❋↴❁↱❋↴❁↱❋↴❁↱❋↴❁↱❋↴❁↱❋↴❁↱❋↴❁↱❋↴❁

I N spite of the fact that three-generation homes are frowned on by the sociologists, they still exist —not so universally as in the years before the establishment of social security and the prevalence of nursing homes and centers for aging citizens, but still in appreciable numbers.

A young social worker of my acquaintance tells with great glee of a conversation she had with her casework supervisor in a family agency. The supervisor took exception to a plan the social worker had proposed for one family which involved a three-generation home.

"What's wrong with having grandparents in the home?" asked the social worker a bit belligerently. "We often had a grandparent with us

—sometimes two at a time. One of my grand-mothers was confined to bed for the last two years of her life—but I don't remember it as any-thing but a positive experience."

The supervisor stared at her unbelievingly. Then she remarked tartly, "All I can say is, your mother must have been a remarkable woman!"

As for me, I have lived happily in three-genera-tion homes belonging to three different genera-tions—the first in my childhood, the second when my own family was growing up, and the third now, in my old age.

There are, of course, many families and situa-tions where three generations could not live to-gether happily. Some old people seem to develop extraordinary skill in being completely unlovable and irritating. Judgmental, complaining, easily offended, self-centered, they seem to acquire a sense of status and importance in proportion to the amount of trouble they stir up. On the other hand, some young people are inconsiderate, re-sentful of criticism, opinionated, impatient of any interference, short-tempered, and basically un-loving.

It seems obvious that people with these personality traits, young and old, cannot live happily
together. Neither, incidentally, can they live happily apart. They simply cannot live happily—
period.

Whenever I think of the difficulties involved
in three-generation homes, I chuckle, remem-
bering an incident that occurred a year or two ago
in a family camp. A group of young parents were
discussing family relationships, and someone
brought up the question of the three-generation
home. The leader had all the answers—he echoed
the opinion of those social workers who condemn
such arrangements as completely impossible. In
the midst of his tirade he suddenly became aware
that my daughter and I (who live together in this
impossible situation) were listening with amusement. He stopped short, embarrassed, but my
daughter rose to the occasion.

"You're quite right," she commented pleasantly. "Having three generations under one roof
does create a number of difficult problems." She
paused a moment, and then added quietly, "*So
does having children*. But no one suggests that we

should stop having children because of the problems."

Given the willingness of all involved to work
together to find solutions for the problems that
arise, a generous amount of love and forgiveness
on both sides, a desire and a willingness on the
part of the grandparents to be useful according
to their capabilities, and genuine gratitude on the
part of the young parents for services rendered,
the chances are good that a three-generation home
will succeed surprisingly well in meeting the
needs of all its various members.

"The Children's People"

‌*⊕↑↓⊕↑*↓⊕↑*↓⊕↑*↓⊕↑↓⊕↑*↓⊕↑*↓⊕↑*↓⊕↑*↓⊕↑*↓⊕

HOW many times I recall with warm and tender amusement something that happened years ago, when my now thirteen-year-old granddaughter was a three-year-old!

She had been teasing her busy mother to read a book to her, and her mother said, "Oh, go ask Gay-Gay. She'll read to you."

So I put aside my knitting, and the toddler and I curled up in a big chair and read the book. When we finished, the child drew a long, satisfied breath and trotted back to her mother, to whom she announced gravely and happily, "Gay-Gay and Grandpa are *the children's people.*"

What an accolade! And what lucky grandparents to be so regarded! But this delightful relationship can be established and maintained only if the grandparents genuinely accept the peripheral position, only if they can happily admit that the responsibility of training the children is first and always the *parents'*!

No two generations ever raise the children in the same way. When grandparents in the home seek to impose *their* rules and *their* restrictions on the children, the results are inevitable: rebellion from the children, resentment from the parents, and hurt feelings for the oldsters.

The wise (but difficult to achieve) attitude is to be always responsive to opportunities to be useful, to enrich the children's lives, to take some of the twenty-four-hour load from the parents, but never to assume responsibility for the children's discipline.

The most helpful contribution a grandparent can make to a troubled family situation, when parents and children are temporarily at loggerheads, is to take himself entirely out of it. Every extra person in such a family crisis adds confusion and irritation. If circumstances make withdrawal impossible (as, for instance, if the family is all together in the car) there is still the *gift of silence*. Adding two cents' worth of advice to reinforce the parent is both unnecessary and unwise. It invites answering back on the part of the children, and distracts their attention from the parents.

Happy the family to which the old people contribute their gift of silence at the appropriate times.

> There is one who keeps silent because
> he has no answer,
> While another keeps silent because
> he knows when to speak.
>
> Ecclesiasticus 20:6

"Guest" Grandparents

❋⟿❂⟿❋⟿❂⟿❋⟿❂⟿❋⟿❂⟿❋⟿❂⟿❋⟿❂⟿❋⟿❂⟿❋⟿❂⟿❋⟿❂⟿❂

I REMEMBER with great joy and tenderness an older couple who often had a meal with us in our home when my three children were growing up.

Our entertaining was always completely informal, "family style." Our guests, to quote my husband, "took us as we were." "What's good enough for us is good enough for them," he used to say.

The Thompsons had been friends of my family for many years. Mr. Thompson had been, before his retirement, the principal of the little public school which my sisters and I attended, so that he had known me from my kindergarten days.

Mrs. Thompson, too, was a friend of long standing. She had been active for years in our Sunday school and had occasionally substituted in the public school.

We had other dinner guests, of course, but the Thompsons stand out in my memory above all others because of the effect they had on our children. Here were two guests whom the children enjoyed as much as we did.

"The Thompsons coming to dinner? Oh, goody!" was the invariable reaction. And because of the children's attitude, I was always relaxed and easy.

After dinner, when the children had been packed off to bed, the four of us grown-ups would settle down to a happy time of friendly talk.

"Florence," one or the other of my guests would be sure to say, "you *do* have the most charming children."

And I would answer, a bit ruefully, "Yes, they were charming tonight. They always are, when you're here. But you should see them sometimes!"

Over the years, I have thought frequently of the Thompsons and have wondered what it was in their approach that brought out the best and most lovable side of my three children, who were, as I very well knew, capable of displaying most unlovable behavior.

Part of the secret, I am sure, was in a basic attitude of acceptance, approval, and pleasant expectation. The Thompsons were completely at ease with children. They both had a direct approach on a man-to-man basis, without affectation or condescension. They were genuinely interested in what the children had to say, and showed their interest by giving their undivided attention. They courteously included the children in the conversation, sometimes stopping to give them a special word of explanation. Their whole attitude and every remark they made showed their affectionate respect for the children *as persons*.

Since I have been a grandparent-in-the-home, I have often wished that I could exert the same beneficent influence that the Thompsons exerted in our home. This was easier to achieve in the days when we were truly house guests, when these visits were a rarity, rose-colored days of family reunion passing all too quickly.

As a member of the family, however, it has become evident to me that there is still the need for the same attitudes that make a successful guest.

Pleasant guests are always outspoken in their appreciation for the hosts' efforts to make them comfortable. Grandparents in the home would do well to make this expression of appreciation a habit.

Understanding guests always build up and reinforce the parents' faith in the genuine lovableness of their children. "Guest" grandparents can serve a high purpose here. When the parents are troubled by a child's discourtesy or misbehavior, what they do *not* need is a sympathetic "Oh, isn't he exasperating! I don't know how you stand it!"

On the contrary, what they really need is reassurance. "Oh, you know this isn't really like him! Usually he's reasonable and more thoughtful." Or maybe "What do you expect of a child his age? This is completely typical behavior. It's a part of growing up." Or maybe even a gentle reminder: "What he needs is just an extra dose of loving. The more unlovable he is, the more he needs it."

Welcome guests are nearly always good listeners. No overworked mother ever has time to listen with undivided attention to all the conversational efforts of all the children all the time. A grandparent, determined to be a courteous "guest," can be a good substitute listener. But will the children accept the grandparent in the role of listener? Only, I feel sure, if the listening grows out of genuine interest; only if the listening is wholehearted and not just a pause until the listener can take over the conversation.

No parent can always be available for reading out loud. A "guest" grandparent, however, can be ready to insert a quiet and relaxing "book time" at appropriate intervals between the periods of normal, noisy activity.

No parent has enough leisure to entertain sick children during the slow days of convalescence, or bored children on stormy days, when the usual occupations lose their charm. A "guest" grandparent who develops a mild passion for games (checkers, dominoes, anagrams, Parcheesi, chess, and so on) may build a relationship with grandchildren that leads to hours of happy companionship through the years, and may, incidentally, be instrumental in helping children to achieve the joy of playing, regardless of victory or defeat.

The idea of being a "guest" grandparent leads to a difficult to achieve, but highly desirable, attitude—a certain degree of detachment. No guest worthy of the name would interfere or become involved in family problems or difficulties, and a "guest" grandparent does well to withdraw to his own room when these inevitable rough spots occur.

The member-of-a-family grandparent who finds it easier to adjust by thinking of himself as a permanent guest, needs to recognize the paradoxical truth that to the family he soon ceases to be a guest, and becomes an accepted and full-fledged member of the group. The more he successfully manages to maintain in his own mind his status as a "guest," the more easily and naturally the family accepts him as a loved and welcome member of the fellowship.

Talking—and Listening

·❋·✧·❋·✧·❋·✧·❋·✧·❋·✧·❋·✧·❋·✧·❋·✧·❋·✧·❋·

W H Y is it that as we grow old, the tendency to chatter becomes well-nigh irresistible? My grandmother, crippled by a broken hip that never healed properly, was for a number of years confined to her room, moving from her bed to an armchair only with great difficulty. She had a sunny disposition, and bore considerable pain with amazing patience and fortitude. And how she loved to talk! Visitors were her chief enjoyment in life.

One of her friends was urging her teenage son to drop in once in a while for a visit. "But I don't know what to talk about!" he objected.

"Talk?" replied his mother. "You won't need to talk—all you'll have to do is *listen!*"

How truly that might be said of many of us! What a tendency we have to run on and on, to add story to story, to hurry to hold our audience with such remarks as "And that reminds me——" or "Another time——" or "But I haven't told you yet——"!

Is this due to the inevitable loneliness of older people? One of the results of the peripheral position is often a feeling of isolation, and perhaps out of this comes the urgency to grasp and hold the center of attention whenever possible, to rebuild our sense of our own importance, to know again the feeling of being listened to with respect.

Unfortunately, too often the results are the opposite of those desired. The chattering older person gets to be a bore, and worsens the isolation against which he is struggling.

There seems to be only one cure for this situation, and it is a difficult one to apply. It is the cultivation of the art of being a good listener. This requires, I think, a genuine acceptance of the peripheral position and a determined transfer of attention from self-centered concerns to the interests of others. Loneliness can be overcome better by relating oneself to others through a real interest in *their* doings and feelings than by determinedly projecting one's own ideas and emotions into the relationship. A good listener is rarely lonely.

In every troubled family situation, moreover, a good listener may prove a healing influence. He may provide a sympathetic, nonjudgmental sounding board, capable of absorbing poured-out feelings of exasperation and frustration, and thus provide a safety valve for the release of tension. Every family should have at least one good listener!

Now about the "good talker." Here we are not going to be concerned with the usual definition: "one who says interesting things in an interesting manner." We are going to make up our own definition: "a good talker is one whose talking is good for the family situation"!

For years I have loved the description of the power of the tongue from the Epistle of James:

If any man offend not in word, the same is a perfect man, and able also to bridle the whole body.

Behold, we put bits in the horses' mouths, that they

may obey us; and we turn about their whole body.

Behold also the ships, which though they be so great, and are driven of fierce winds, yet are they turned about with a very small helm, whithersoever the governor listeth.

Even so the tongue is a little member, and boasteth great things. Behold, how great a matter a little fire kindleth! . . .

For every kind of beasts, and of birds, and of serpents, and of things in the sea, is tamed, and hath been tamed of mankind:

But the tongue can no man tame; it is an unruly evil, full of deadly poison.

James 3:2–8 KJV

We are thinking here of a "good" talker as one who is constantly striving to control his unruly tongue, who recognizes its potential for spreading poison, and also its potential for healing; deliberately, with conscious determination, he seeks to use this peculiarly powerful instrument for the "good" of family life.

Do you remember the fairy story "Toads and Diamonds"? The beautiful and unappreciated maiden goes to the well to fetch water, and is accosted by a poor old woman (a good fairy in disguise), who asks her for a drink of water.

The maiden complies graciously, and because of her kindness is given a gift: from then on, at every word she speaks, a flower or a jewel will drop from her lips. Upon her return home, her amazed and delighted stepmother hastens to send her own ill-tempered daughter to the well, hoping that she, too, may be the recipient of such amazing good fortune. But the girl finds no poor old woman at the well. Instead, a proud and imperious princess demands a drink. The girl answers insolently, and *her* reward is that from then on, at every word she speaks, toads and vipers fall from her lips.

Toads and diamonds! What a deep truth is hidden in this pictorial tale—and surely it is a truth especially needed by those of us with three-quarters of a century of living behind us. Too many of us, as we grow older, become tart and bitter, and complaining, whining words spread their ugliness all around us. Few of us have the grace to guard our lips so that consideration for others, gratitude, appreciation, and love fill our surroundings with spiritual treasure and scatter everywhere the subtle fragrance of loving kindness.

Mealtimes

A T no time, perhaps, in the twenty-four hours of the day is the difference in child training between the generations more noticeable than at mealtime.

Who now, for instance, would dream of expecting a modern child to speak only when he's spoken to, or who would correct an overtalkative youngster at the dinner table with the reminder that children should be seen, and not heard? Those days, for good or bad, are gone forever.

For many grandparents, however, the echo of such restrictions still lingers in their consciousness from their childhood days and, to a lesser degree, from the days when their children were growing up.

Something in an old person's make-up reacts with voluble chatter to the relaxation of a good meal and a more or less captive audience. Food also, apparently, relaxes children's tongues, and sometimes the insistent competition for a tired mother's attention causes tension and irritability. Few of us oldsters have learned the skill of sandwiching in brief comments that form no real interruption to the family chatter. Usually, when a grandparent speaks, there seems to be an expectation—almost, indeed, a demand—that all conversation stop; and many meals could easily be dominated by an endless monologue. It is revealing to be aware of our own reaction, for instance, to a child's thoughtless interruption of an adult conversation. Most of us resent it, and are apt to show our resentment in subtle (and not so subtle) ways.

To be aware of this mealtime problem is to be part way to a solution. Tactful grandparents will consciously accept their role as onlookers at the family table, will firmly limit their table conversation to brief comments that do not carry after them a whole train of attached incidents, will try to earn the reputation of being good listeners, and will accept, without resentment, inattention and interruptions.

It is even possible that, recognizing the difficulties, grandparents might prefer to have most of their meals apart from the rest of the family. A rare grandparent might earn the gratitude of a harassed mother by suggesting this arrangement himself. "Look, let me have a tray in my room (or out on the porch, or in the library); I'm in the middle of a chapter I want to read," or "I'm tired and I'd like to be quiet."

Sometimes, in homes where this procedure has been worked out, the grandparent becomes a specially invited "guest" for a meal. Sometimes, too, one of the grandchildren will demand, "I want my dinner on a tray too. I'll eat with grandfather tonight!"

Do you remember the old fable of the narrow-necked jar? The more of its contents the inserted hand tried to grasp, the less could be withdrawn. There is a parallel here: Grandparents who are grasping and demanding, defeat their own purposes and increase their loneliness and bitterness.

When they cease demanding, and remain pleasantly and responsively aloof, much of what they really want comes to them without any effort on their part.

P. S. If I were writing to parents instead of to grandparents, I might be inclined to make a different emphasis.

The other day I was walking with my six-year-old grandson through a field of goldenrod, following a rough path almost completely overgrown. The path led downhill, and the going was fairly difficult. Suddenly I stepped in a hole and sat down in an ungraceful heap.

"Are you all right?" asked Ted, anxiously.

And when I assured him I was not hurt, he held out his hand to help me to my feet. And for the rest of the walk he showed a new awareness of my limitations.

"Be careful, Gay-Gay," he cautioned. "There's a big stone here," and "Watch out for the briers," and "Here's a log across the path. Can you step over it?"

I should like to remind parents that exposure to the feebleness and the idiosyncrasies of old age is obviously the only way young people can develop that consideration and courtesy toward elderly people which is so charming. The presence of grandparents in the home is a priceless opportunity to develop in the children the very understandings and responses which will add blessedness to the years ahead (and not so far ahead at that), when the parents themselves will be "the old people."

Children who have been trained to affectionate tolerance for the foibles of their grandparents are far more apt to prove understanding and accepting of their own parents in their declining years.

Response to Need

ONE of the insights that comes with the passing years is that few satisfactions can compare with the awareness of having been instrumental in meeting some human need. When as Christians we are instructed to love our neighbors as ourselves, the resultant joy is rarely mentioned; and yet it is truly one of the deep and rewarding satisfactions of life.

The toddler who cheerfully picks up his toys and finds himself caught up in a warm hug and hears an enthusiastic "Thank you, darling. That's a real help!" is beginning to learn this important lesson.

The older child, helping with household

chores, running errands, baby-sitting with a younger child, needs to hear over and over again, "Oh, thank you, dear. Whatever would I do without such a helpful big sister in the family?"

And the teenager, entering into family consultations, accepting some necessary sacrifice because of limited financial means or giving up some long-awaited treat because of a family emergency, has earned the right to warm praise and appreciation: "I *knew* we could depend on you."

All these early experiences are important preparation for adult life. The young couple just starting their life together will build the foundations of their marriage most strongly if they have both learned, through innumerable experiences of this kind, the joy of meeting another's need. Too frequently, hopes of married happiness are dashed because each is seeking his own fulfillment, and then the partner becomes only a thing to be used, not a loved person to be joyously served.

Parents find joy in meeting the needs of helpless infants, and their understanding of the child's changing needs grows and deepens as the child grows. And those of us who have lived active lives, working at tasks that seem to us significant, have many precious memories of the deep joy that comes when something we have said or done has been of use to someone else.

Probably one of the bitterest feelings that comes with old age is the feeling of being of no further use, incapable of the joy of meeting needs. No person, however, is ever so completely isolated as to be untouched by any human need. Sometimes we allow the contracting circles of life to harden into a wall behind which we hide, immersed in our own needs, oblivious to the needs of the people around us. But although in old age our contacts are few, our responsibility to meet human need still exists. Erich Fromm reminds us that the basic definition of responsibility is the *ability to respond,* and that is an ability we can cherish and cultivate to the end of our lives.

Even though the contracting circles have crowded us into a sickroom, we still have a number of contacts.

First of all comes the family. If we are ill at home, we know from past experience what an added burden this means. That it is a burden willingly and lovingly borne is good reason for upwelling gratitude on our part. Is there nothing our family needs from *us* in this situation?

One thing is sure—bewailing the fact that we are such a care and of no use to anybody does not help. Nor does complaining about unavoidable discomfort and pain. Far better is an attitude of acceptance. (There's that word again: we can't get away from it.) This is a time for the cultivation of sincere and gracious expressions of appreciation for the countless services rendered. The family needs, and is entitled to, the satisfaction of knowing that we are grateful and contented.

What is true of the family is true of friends. When busy people take time out to visit us, either at home or in the hospital, what do they need from us? Surely not a detailed listing of aches and pains and gruesome details of sickbed routines. Maybe they need a friendly ear to listen to *their* troubles. Maybe they need, even more than we do, a few minutes of genuine love and concern focused on them.

Then there is the nurse. With what patient energy she steadily pursues her work of service! What does she need from us? At least courtesy and the refraining from unnecessary demands. Maybe, also, recognition of her as a person, a focusing on her rather than ourselves, or a well-earned compliment.

And here comes the doctor. How long is it since he had an uninterrupted night's sleep? What a burden he carries constantly on his heart: the pain his skill is powerless to relieve, the tragedies and heartaches he cannot avert. Is there anything he needs from us? Certainly appreciation is never amiss. Perhaps this morning he also needs an affectionate recognition of his weariness, and maybe even an extra bit of courage on our part to bear necessary pain uncomplainingly and so make his task easier.

Many of us in our illness look forward to visits from a beloved minister. We know we need him and the strength and comfort we catch from his contagious faith. But perhaps, more than we realize, he needs something from us: a demonstration of the power of religion to strengthen and make joyous even the bitter experiences of life.

Surely it is true that no matter how contracted the circles may be, no matter how few personal contacts we may have, while life lasts, no one of us is relieved from our responsibility to minister to the needs of others. One other important thing needs to be said: this particular ministry can be performed by no one else; it is an individual assignment, nontransferable.

Usefulness

EVERYONE wants to be useful. But men's ways of evaluating usefulness are probably very different from God's ways. Useful—for what? That question probes the depths of your whole philosophy of life. You cannot answer it adequately without facing the meaning of life itself.

Our age is witnessing innumerable instances of tragic loss of life. Violence and bloodshed in Vietnam—thousands of young lives snuffed out. Starvation in India—children dying before they have a chance to live. Racism in Africa and in America. What a sorry mess the world is in! What is the use of it all?

Faith declares, in contradiction to this seeming

futility, that life *has* purpose—dimly sensed, almost completely hidden from the searching souls of men, but indubitably woven into the fabric of life itself.

Suppose that part of God's purpose is the creation of human souls capable of entering into the world's suffering and injecting into it the only possible redemptive force—love.

How could such a purpose be fulfilled without those who suffer? If there were no illness, no weakness, no helplessness, no suffering, how could human beings ever know helpfulness, sympathy, compassion, self-sacrificing love?

Useful—in the final years of inactivity? Useful —in weeks and months of illness? Useful—when failing sight and hearing make you a burden to others? Useful—when all you have to look forward to is death?

Yes—an unequivocal yes to all these questions. God can use every dedicated soul for his eternal purposes, no matter how erroneously men's judgment declares its uselessness. All that is necessary is the willingness to be used.

A dear Scottish grandmother I knew used to

tell of one such dedicated soul. "One day I went
to see Ann. She was very ill indeed, quite near
the end of a long battle with tuberculosis, but she
was cheerful and relaxed. Wracked by fits of
coughing, she squeezed my hand in welcome.
'Ah, Libby,' she said quietly, after one specially
violent paroxysm of coughing, 'when I was
young, I ran here and there at the Lord's bidding,
and now he says to me: "Ann! Lie there and
cough!" and so—I lie here and cough.' "

Most of us dread long, drawn-out illness, not
so much, perhaps, because of the possible physical suffering involved for ourselves as because of
the dread of being a burden on those we love.

But what if this burden, lovingly borne, may be
the very means through which these loved ones
grow in patience, in spiritual strength, in human
compassion.

What if the example of helplessness and suffering, bravely and cheerfully endured, may be exactly what is needed to bring new depths of understanding and new challenges to courageous
living to those who stand by?

Who can fathom the mysteries of the interaction of human relationships? How often do we echo the poet's thought: "God moves in a mysterious way/His wonders to perform."

Milton in his blindness caught a clear insight when he declared: "They also serve/Who only stand and wait."

For God's eternal purposes, no dedicated soul is ever useless.

Death

*ゃ•◈ヶゃ◈ゃゃ◈ゃ*ゃ◈ゃ*ゃ◈ゃ*ゃ◈ゃ*ゃ◈ゃ*ゃ◈ゃ*ゃ◈*

NO consideration of old age can be realistic without dealing with the imminence of death. That is one reality with which every old person, sooner or later, must come to grips.

Of course, long before we have reached the three-quarters of a century mark, we have had innumerable experiences with the death of others. But our own death is something else again.

The fear of death itself is hard to understand. All our experience points to the fact that the actual passing from life to death is usually nothing to dread.

How precious to most of us is a peaceful night's sleep! How fortunate we are to be able to say,

"Ah, I slept so well last night!" It is one of our chief desires and delights. So if death really is what it seems to be—the end of all consciousness, a deep and eternal sleep free from all pain and anxiety—who, having lived to a ripe old age and knowing that inevitably only greater weariness, feebleness, and suffering lie ahead, could fail to welcome death as a friend? Who could dread the painless peace of eternal nothingness?

In some ways, many of us today are more fortunate than our ancestors. Few today face in death the dread of eternal fire and brimstone. Surely it must have been the most worthy and sensitive souls who, because of their greater awareness of "sin," suffered most in this belief. Now, fortunately, the dread of hell fire no longer adds its torment to the deathbed. How strange that the belief in eternal punishment should so long have survived side by side with the irreconcilable conviction of a loving God!

Changing points of view, however, have not only removed the fear of hell fire; they have also, to some degree, removed the comfort of the hope of immortality. Many people nowadays see death as the end of individual human personality.

Who is wise enough to give final answers to the

riddle of the ages? Who can honestly hold any
belief save an open-minded agnosticism?

It is easy to see why many of the "God is dead"
group have discarded the belief in the continu-
ance of individuality after death. For the Christian emphasis on the worth of the individual
seems correlative to the Christian belief in a loving Father-Creator to whom each person is precious; and without that emphasis, the destruction
of individuality seems of as little consequence as
the destruction of the body.

Science itself, however, has given us a different
conception of destruction. There is, it appears, no
such thing.

We put water in a pot and set it on the burner.
After a while, the water disappears. Have we
destroyed the water? Not at all. We have merely
changed it into vapor.

The green leaves of summer turn brown and
shrivel up. They fall from the tree to the ground.
They are drenched by the rain and snow, trodden
underfoot, and crushed to powder. But are they
destroyed? We know they are not; they are
merely changed. Their usefulness is far from
over. The rich dust will provide food for other
leaves on other trees, *ad infinitum*.

We tear up a piece of paper. Have we destroyed it? Not really. We have changed it into a handful of scraps. We burn the scraps, but we have only reduced them to ashes.

Even so evanescent and fragile a thing as a candle flame apparently escapes total destruction.

Sir Arthur Keith is one of the great British scientists. Professor Arthur Compton is one of the great American scientists. The first is an utter disbeliever; the second a thorough believer. According to Sir Arthur Keith, when a man dies he goes out like a candle; to which Professor Compton replies that the candle does not go out; its energy goes on and on to the farthest reaches of the universe. Be sure of this: If God is, one way or another our candle does not go out. Its mode of going on may be utterly different from anything we have pictured it to be. Indeed, I am sure that must be so, but one way or another, as Emerson said:

> ". . . What is excellent,
> As God lives, is permanent."

and in manners and fashions beyond our power to imagine the candle does not go out.*

* Harry Emerson Fosdick, "Life's Candle Does Not Go Out," in Stanley I. Stuber and Thomas C. Clark, eds., *Treasury of the Christian Faith* (New York: Association Press, 1949), p. 425.

If, then, destruction, even of physical matter, really is *not* destruction at all, but merely transformation, what shall we think of the endurance of reality that is not physical?

Is there any such reality? Or shall we believe that *all* there is to this beloved minister who has spread the blessing of contagious, joyous faith to hundreds of people is his body? Absurd! Or this mother, whose years have been a continuous self-sacrifice to provide for her family—is her body all there is to her?

Many of us hold to the belief that in some mysterious and inexplicable way, personality is *more* than the mere physical body which clothes it, and so we entertain, frankly and without embarrassment, the hope that this human personality, this spiritual reality, may prove to be as indestructible as matter.

To risk an oversimplification, it seems to me that two possibilities, and only two, exist. Either God (eternal Mind and Purpose) exists in the universe, or he does not.

If he does not, then the sooner this sorry world blows itself to bits, the better. Who would really care to continue to live, and to bring children into the world with the belief that

Life's but a walking shadow . . .
     It is a tale
Told by an idiot, full of sound and fury,
Signifying nothing.

William Shakespeare
Macbeth V, v, 17

If, on the other hand, God does exist, all the materialists' furore of arguing and denying cannot alter the fact. Nor would the total destruction of this world by scientific or power-mad lunatics change the eternal truth one iota.

Both belief in God and belief in his nonexistence leave deep questions unanswered, but the questions are very different. Belief in God raises the problem of evil in all its varied forms—injustice, hatred, cruelty, man's inhumanity to man, racism, greed, selfishness, treachery, war, persecution, violence—the list is endless. And all attempted answers seem inadequate.

But the belief in God's nonexistence, the "God is dead" philosophy, raises questions also. How account for those undeniable instances where man has attained to exalted heights of spiritual living? Or for those hundreds and thousands of nameless people who have lived quiet lives of gentle goodness and loving kindness?

Why did Jane Addams give up her comfortable life to struggle among the poor and under-privileged people of Chicago?

Why did Albert Schweitzer condemn himself to a life of struggle and hardship, to bring medical help to people he had never known?

Why did Martin Niemoller oppose the powerful Nazi regime at imminent risk of martyrdom?

Why did Dietrich Bonhoeffer, having found asylum in America, deliberately return to Germany, knowing that certain execution awaited him?

Why does Martin Luther King throw himself wholeheartedly into the civil rights struggle, risking assassination daily, almost hourly, from those, even among his own people, who oppose his nonviolent stand?

Why did the young Jesus, his heart aflame with love for sinning, suffering men, deliberately "set his face to go to Jerusalem" and endure the torture and humiliation of the Cross?

How account for what Harry Kemp calls "the upward reach in the heart of man"?

If Christianity has no adequate answer to the problem of *evil,* scientific materialism has no answer to the problem of *good.*

For myself, I choose to believe that God exists. I have had far too much of goodness, and truth, and love in my life to doubt it; and I find no scientific explanation for these eternal realities. And because I believe in God, I have hope that the creatures he has created share in his nature and are indestructible.

I shall die, then, fully expecting some indefinable, indescribable continuation of life, in which I shall still be recognizably myself—although I would hope for infinite possibilities of improvement!

If I'm right, a goodly number of scientific materialists are going to find themselves gloriously surprised in the hereafter! And if I'm wrong, I'll never have the chagrin of hearing the disbelievers declare, "I told you so."

Two wise old men have contributed to this faith of mine. The first is John Quincy Adams.

One day when John Quincy Adams was eighty years of age a friend met him on the streets of Boston. "How is John Quincy Adams?" this friend asked gaily. The old man's eyes began to twinkle, and then he spoke slowly. His words have become classic. "John Quincy Adams himself is very well, thank you. But the house he lives in is sadly dilapidated. It is tottering on its foundations. The walls are badly shattered, and the roof is worn. The building trembles with every wind, and I think John Quincy Adams will have to move out of it before long. But he himself is very well." And with a wave of the hand the old man walked on.*

The second is Benjamin Franklin. Here is his epitaph, as he wrote it:

> The Body of BENJAMIN FRANKLIN,
> Printer,
> Like the Covering of an old Book,
> Its Contents torn out,
> And stript of its Lettering and Gilding,
> Lies here, Food for Worms;
> But the Work shall not be lost,
> It will (as he believed) appear once more,
> In a new and more beautiful Edition,
> Corrected and amended
> By the Author.**

* J. G. Gilkey, "Old Age and Immortality," in *Treasury of the Christian Faith,* Stanley I. Stuber and Thomas C. Clark, eds. (New York: Association Press, 1949), p. 421.
** Charles L. Wallis, ed., *Stories on Stone: A Book of American Epitaphs* (New York: Oxford University Press, 1954), p. 137.